Moth

NOVALIS

In the beginning

" *By blood, I am Albanian.*
By citizenship, an Indian.

By faith, I am a Catholic nun.
As to my calling, I belong to
the world.

As to my heart, I belong entirely to the Heart of Jesus."

Her name was Gonxha Agnes Bojaxhiu.

She was the youngest child of Nikola and Dronda Bojaxhiu.

She was born on August 26, 1910, in Skopje, in the Balkans.

She had a sister named Aga and a brother named Lazar.

Her father died when she was around eight years old.

When she was eighteen, she decided to become a missionary. In September 1928, she entered the Loreto Sisters, in Ireland.

She was given the name Sister Mary Teresa, in honour of St. Theresa of Lisieux, who had been canonized three years earlier.

She left for India in December 1928, and arrived in Calcutta on January 6, 1929.

After making her first vows in May 1931, Sister Teresa taught young girls at St. Mary's School in Entally, a suburb of Calcutta.

On May 24, 1937, Sister Teresa made her final vows. From that moment on, she was known as Mother Teresa.

She kept teaching at St. Mary's and became principal of the school in 1944.

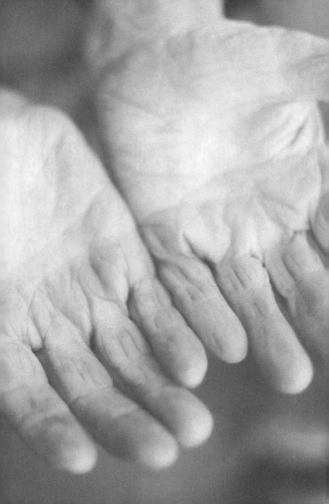

The call
within the call

On September 10, 1946, she boarded a train for Darjeeling, in northern India, near the Chinese border, to make her annual retreat.

T his journey would change her life.

That day, Mother Teresa experienced what she described as her "call within the call."

The words of Jesus on the cross – "I am thirsty" (John 19:28) – took root in her.

She discovered the depth of God's thirst. The thirst of love for all people. The thirst to go and meet each person, especially the poorest of the poor.

Satisfying this thirst became her main goal.

She devoted her entire life to it.

Weeks and months went by.

This inner thirst was getting bigger and bigger.

Jesus spoke to her and revealed to her his heart's desire to have "victims of love" who "would spread his love to others."

He was suffering because of the indifference being shown to the poor and his desire to be loved by them.

"Come, be my light."

"I cannot go there on my own," he told her.

The way forward would be a radical one: leaving everything behind to serve the poorest of the poor.

Two years later, on August 17, 1948, she put on her white sari with the blue border for the first time and left her convent.

Like a bride ready to be wedded to poverty.

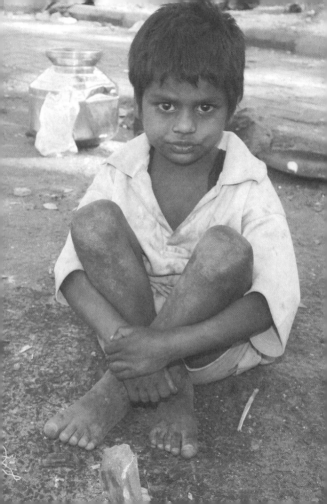

A

universal

vocation

*I*n truth, Mother Teresa
was God's gift to the
poorest of the poor.

*In Mother Teresa's smile, words
and deeds, Jesus again walked the
streets of the world as the Good
Samaritan.*

John Paul II

S he imposed a strict discipline on herself. Each day began with the Eucharist.

Then, rosary in hand, she went to meet the one she had received in the sacrament

She found him in the rejected, the unloved, the neglected.

December 21, 1948: her first visit to the slums.

She met a few families, washed the sores of a few children, cared for a sick old man lying in the street and a woman with tuberculosis who was starving to death.

*A*bove all, we want the dying to feel wanted; we want them to know that there are people who love them, who really want them, at least in these last few hours that remain to them, to know human and divine love. To know that they, too, are children of God, that they have not been forgotten, that they are loved, that they matter and that young people are there to serve them.

It is through our hands that the poor need to be served; it is through our hearts that they need to be loved. The religion of Christ is love, the contagion of love. I wouldn't touch a leper for a thousand pounds, yet I willingly care for him for the love of God.

After a few months, some of her former students joined her.

On October 7, 1950, the congregation of the Missionaries of Charity was officially founded in the Archdiocese of Calcutta.

By the early 1960s, Mother Teresa was sending her sisters to other parts of India.

Houses would later open in Venezuela, Rome, Tanzania, and eventually on every continent.

Over the years, Mother Teresa would also open houses in almost every communist country, including the former Soviet Union, Albania and Cuba.

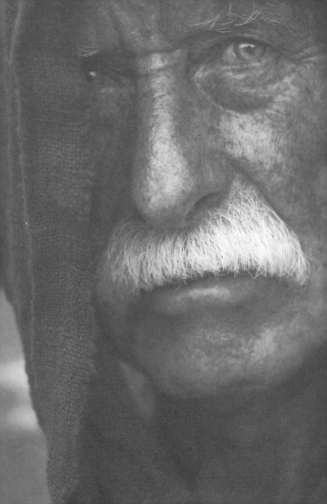

Serving
the poor

The life of Mother Teresa was given entirely to serving the poor. She tended to their physical needs, but also to their spiritual needs.

She tried above all to restore to each person dignity, importance, a sense of joy.

The poor are thirsting for water [but also] for peace, truth and justice. The poor are naked, [they need] clothing, human dignity and compassion for sinners.

I will never forget the man I picked
up off the street one day. He was
covered in vermin. His face was the
only clean part of him. And yet
this man, after we brought him to
our home for the dying, said this:

"I lived like an animal in the
street, but I will die like an angel,
loved and cared for." And he died
wonderfully well. He entered his
home with God, for death is simply
going home to God's house.

It was because he had experienced this love, because he had felt wanted and loved, had felt that he was important to someone, that, in his final moments, he felt this joy in his life.

L ove for the poor comes from seeing their misery, their anguish.

Can we really know our poor,
especially those who are here?
Maybe they are in our own
families. For charity begins at
home. Do we know them? Do we
know those who are alone, left out,
forgotten?

What I want from you is this:
when we look together and see the
poor within our own families, we
begin to love at home, to the
point of suffering out of love. I
want us to always be ready to
smile, to find a way to spend
time with our loved ones.

If we know them, we know that the poor is our neighbour, someone who lives with us. We are aware of them. Do we know those around us? The poor hunger for bread, for rice, but also for love and for the living Word of God.

Serving the poor is therefore not our ultimate goal, but a way to make concrete our love for Christ.

That is why we owe the poor such deep gratitude. That is why they are humanity's hope for salvation.

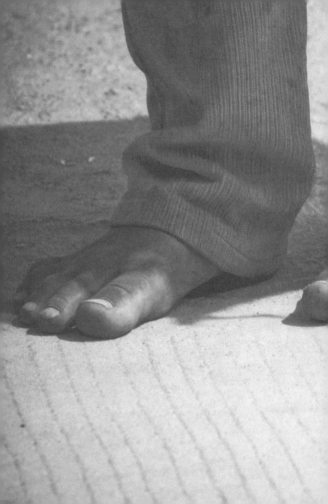

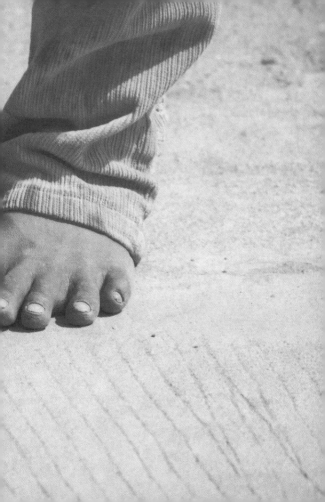

One with Christ

For Mother Teresa, every act we do for the poor has meaning only if it is deeply rooted in our oneness with Christ.

We are nuns. Our vocation is not to work with lepers or the dying; our vocation is to belong to Jesus. Because I belong to Him, this work is a way for me to live my love for Him in action. This is not an end, but a means. Because my vocation is to belong to Him absolutely, to love Him with an indivisible love and chastity, I make these vows.

Love to pray throughout the day, feel the need to pray often, and take the trouble to pray.

Prayer opens up the heart so it is big enough to hold the gift of Himself that God gives us. Ask and seek, and your heart will grow big enough to welcome God and make Him your own.

We must be aware of being one with Christ, as He was aware of being one with his Father.

In the poor, we truly touch the body of Christ. In the poor, it is a starving Christ whom we feed, it is Christ whom we dress, and it is the homeless Christ whom we shelter.

Our hearts must be full of love for Him and, because this love must express itself in action, it is clear that the poorest of the poor allow us to express this love for God. Governments do a lot to help the poor. We offer something else: the love of Christ.

P rayer and the eucharist were at the centre of her life and everything she did.

Jesus made himself the "Bread of Life" to satisfy our desire for love. He became the one who is hungry, who is naked, who has no shelter, to give us the opportunity to transform our love for Him into concrete actions towards the poor.

What blood is for the body, prayer is for the soul…

I get my strength from God through prayer… Prayer also gives us all the joy we need to do what we have to do.

Union with Christ
produces a fruit that is
beyond compare: joy.

Never let sadness overwhelm you to the point that you forget the joy of the risen Lord, the Christ who gives Himself to us in the Eucharist and in the poor.

We must be able to radiate the joy of Christ and express it through our actions. If our actions are useful but not joyful, our poor people could never rise up and hear God, for we want to call to them and tell them to draw near to Him. We want them to feel that they are loved.

If we go and see them with sadness in our faces, we will only increase their despair. Often it is not things they need. The worst illness a person can have is feeling unwanted.

Our goal is to be with them with helping hands, loving hearts, and to see Christ in them.

In our community, we often tell
Our Lady that she is the cause of
our Joy, because she gave us Jesus.

May we become the cause of her
joy, because we give Jesus to others.

Stay close to Jesus, with a smile on your face.

*The poor who are homeless need
shelter made of bricks, but also of
a joyful heart that understands
them, enfolds them, loves them.
They are sick and need medical
care, but they also need a helping
hand and a friendly smile.*

The excluded, those who have been rejected, who are unloved, the alcoholics, the dying, those who are alone and abandoned, the marginalized, the untouchables, and the lepers; all those who are a burden for human society, who have lost all hope and faith in life, who have forgotten how to smile, who no longer know what it is to receive a little human warmth, a loving and friendly gesture: these are the ones who turn to us to be comforted.

If we turn our backs on them, we turn our backs on Christ!

The dark
night of the
soul

One aspect of her spiritual life would not be revealed until after her death: she called it "darkness" – the painful experience that accompanied her all her life, the sense of being separated from God.

My smile is a cloak that covers a lot of pain. Smiling all the time. The Sisters and the people think that my faith, my hope, my love fill me with great joy, and the intimacy with God and union with His will permeate my heart. If they only knew.

I feel that God is not God, that He doesn't really exist. There is a terrible darkness within me. As if everything were dead within me, for all is frozen.

It's only blind faith that carries me, because to be honest, all is darkness for me.

Sometimes the agony and desolation are so deep, and great hope for the Absent one is so profound, the only prayer I can still manage to say is "Sacred Heart of Jesus, I place my trust in You. I will satisfy your thirst for souls."

Today I felt deep joy: because Jesus can no longer experience agony directly, He wants to experience it through me. I give myself up to Him more than ever.

Life in abundance

What matters is not what we give, but the love with which we give.

Because Christ is invisible, we cannot show him our love. But our neighbours are always visible and we can do for them what we would like to do for Him if he were visible.

Every person is Christ for me, and because there is only one Jesus, that person is, in that moment, the only person in the world.

Holiness is not the luxury of the few; it is a simple duty, for you and for me.

Keep the light of Christ burning in your heart always, for He alone is the path to follow. He is the Life to live. He is the Love to love. Our labours are merely an expression of our love for Christ.

If you can't feed a hundred people,
feed at least one.

She was awarded the Nobel Peace Prize in 1979 and accepted it on behalf of the poor. She took advantage of this opportunity to make a passionate appeal:

Just get together, love one another, bring that peace, that joy, that strength of presence of each other in the home. And we will be able to overcome all the evil that is in the world.

There is so much suffering, so much hatred, so much misery, and we with our prayer, with our sacrifice are beginning at home. Love begins at home, and it is not how much we do, but how much love we put in the action that we do. It is to God Almighty – how much we do it does not matter, because He is infinite, but how much love we put in that action. How much we do to Him in the person that we are serving.

I want you to find the poor here, right in your own home first. And begin love there. Be that good news to your own people. And find out about your next-door neighbour — do you know who they are?

I believe that love begins at home, and if we can create a home for the poor, I think that more and more love will spread. And we will be able through this understanding love to bring peace, be the good news to the poor. The poor in our own family first, in our country and in the world.

God has created us in His image and likeness, enabling us to know Him, love Him and serve Him in this world, so as to be happy with Him forever in the life to come. This is the true purpose of life. To live our lives with this aim, our lives must be woven with prayer.

*What I can do, you cannot.
What you can do, I cannot. But
together we can do something
beautiful for God.*

*Yes, you must live life beautifully
and not allow the spirit of the
world that makes gods out of
power, riches, and pleasure make
you to forget that you have been
created for greater things — to love
and be loved.*

She died on September 5, 1997.

The other day I dreamed that I was standing before the gates of paradise. St. Peter said to me, "Go back to earth; there are no slums here."

Mother Teresa of Calcutta was beatified on October 19, 2003, in Rome by Pope John Paul II.

We can't do great things, just ordinary things with great love.

© 2013 Novalis Publishing Inc.

Cover: Quatre-Quarts
Cover photo: © Crestock.com
Layout: Danielle Dugal and Amy Eaton
Interior photos: © Crestock.com, except for p. 7, p. 17 & p. 102 (W.P. Wittman)
Translation: Anne Louise Mahoney

Works and websites consulted:
A Chain of Love: Mother Teresa and Her Suffering Disciples, by Kathryn Spinks (SPCK, 1984)
Come Be My Light, by Mother Teresa (Doubleday, 2009)
In the Silence of the Heart, by Kathryn Spink (SPCK, 1983)
Mère Teresa: Sa vie, ses combats, ses paroles, by Xavier Lecoeur (Bayard Jeunesse, 2006)
Pensées spirituelles, by José Louis González-Balado (Mediaspaul, 2005)
Prier 15 jours avec mère Teresa, by Francesco Follo (Nouvelle Cité, 2003)
http://www.motherteresa.org
http://www.nobelprize.org
http://www.vatican.va

Originally published in French by Les Éditions Novalis in 2010.

Published by Novalis

Publishing Office	Head Office
10 Lower Spadina Avenue, Suite 400	4475 Frontenac Street
Toronto, Ontario, Canada	Montréal, Québec, Canada
M5V 2Z2	H2H 2S2

www.novalis.ca

Library and Archives Canada Cataloguing in Publication

Mother Teresa / Anne Louise Mahoney, translator.

(Faith moments) Translation of: Mère Teresa. ISBN 978-2-89646-485-2

1. Teresa, Mother, 1910-1997. 2. Nuns--India--Calcutta--
Biography. 3. Missionaries of Charity--Biography. I. Mahoney,
Anne Louise II. Series: Faith moments

BX4406.5.Z8M6613 2013   271'.97   C2012-901602-0

Printed in Canada.

We acknowledge the financial support of the Government of Canada through
the Canada Book Fund for business development activities.

5   4   3   2   1   17   16   15   14   13